# GIN WORLD #2020

The Gin Book with Classic and Modern
Cocktail Recipes for Every Occasion

**August McGillmann**

# TABLE OF CONTENTS

*Welcome to Gin World #2020- The Gin Book with Classic and Modern Cocktail Recipes for Every Occasion! This book is here to educate you on all things gin, from its medicinal beginnings to the new age gin revival. Our comprehensive detailing of the (g)ins and outs of this centuries old drink will impress friends, family, and probably your local bartender! But, you won't only learn the intricacies of gin theory- we've also included a comprehensive collection of cocktail classics and recipe renegades to put the theory into practice. Put your wine aside and pour flavoured vodkas down the sink; gin is here and it's making its mark!*

# HOW IS GIN DEFINED?

You can't have gin without juniper berries, period. It is the addition of juniper (and then other botanical flavourings) that lend gin its characteristically earthy and fragrant flavour. The addition of juniper berries to the distillation (or redistillation) process results in an aromatic flavour akin to that of a spruce or pine tree- imagine the smell of a Christmas tree, and you've got the right idea!

The EU legally categorises gin in 4 different ways, with all ethanol and spirits coming from agricultural origins:

• **Juniper-flavoured spirit drinks**
*fermented grain mash that undergoes pot distillation to a moderate ABV (eg. 65%), prior to a redistillation process featuring additional botanical flavours. This resulting in a twice distilled beverage infused with herbal flavour compounds, with a minimum of 30% ABV*

• **Gin**
*juniper and other natural flavouring substances are added to a pre-distilled neutral spirit. The beverage must meet a minimum of 37.5% ABV and have juniper as its predominant flavour*

• **Distilled Gin**
*ethanol of agricultural origin and an ABV of 96% is distilled in traditional gin stills, and with the addition of juniper berries and other botanicals. Juniper must be the predominant flavour (with-*

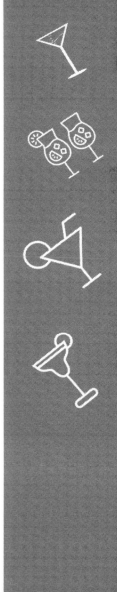

out the use of artificial flavourings or essences), and a minimum ABV of 37.5%

### • London (Dry) Gin

*a maximum methanol content of 5g/hectolitre of ABV 100% equivalent ethanol is essential, and flavour must be infused through re-distillation in traditional gin stills, resulting in a beverage of 70% ABV. Only water, and 0.1g sugar/litre of the final product may be added, with a minimum strength of 37.5% ABV and juniper as the predominant flavour*

As you can see, the running theme in any definition of gin is the predominant flavouring of juniper berries. Prior to this infusion of flavour one can classify gin as vodka- they both have the same basic constituents and initial distillation process; it is the redistillation and/or juniper berry infusion elevates gin to an independent spirit drink. It can be argued that gin is a flavoured vodka, but vodka can never fall under the classification of a gin.

# THE HISTORY OF GIN

It's taken many centuries to perfect the gin we have available to us today. Despite gaining recognition as a quintessentially British drink, gin actually started out around Belgium and Holland. As early as the 13th century there is reference to a 'jenever'* flavoured spirit (jenever being the Dutch word for juniper), and by the 16th century recipes for such a drink had been printed.

To start with there are merely sporadic references to jenever/gin in various texts, but come the early to mid-17th century the drink was quickly gaining popularity. Dutch and Flemish breweries were redistilling malted barley spirit and malt wine with juniper berries and other botanicals before distributing it to pharmacies where it was sold as a medicinal tonic- the spirit was seen as a remedy for ailments such as gout, gallstones, and a range of stomach and kidney health problems.

It was in this period that gin started making its way to the British Isles. The Dutch connection from King William III is likely to have played a role in the beverage's growing popularity, as was the heavy taxing of imported spirits such as French brandy. The government then allowed unlicensed production of the spirit, and so it naturally became a cheap and easily obtainable alcoholic alternative.

Gin became the poor-man's drink. The unregulated brewing

---

\* We've written it here as 'jenever' in line with the earliest written references, but nowadays this gin variation is more commonly known as 'genever'

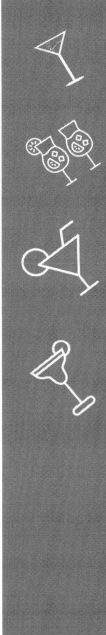

allowed use of otherwise unfit grains to create a drink that was cheap, accessible, and strong. These combined factors resulted in a period known as 'The Gin Craze'. This period ran from 1695-1735 and featured the creation of thousands of establishments that existed solely on the consumption of gin. The drink was seen unfavourably for a long time (where do you think the nickname 'mother's ruin' came from?), and credited with the surge of serious social issues, and the flattening of London's growing population rates. Having quickly lost favour with the ruling British classes they implemented raised taxes and distribution laws, these being the Gin Acts of 1736 and 1751, respectively.

As 'The Gin Craze' quietened and the drink regained some of its lost credibility different forms of gin began to establish themselves. Jenever was being produced in the Netherlands throughout the period of British upheaval, but the two spirits could no longer be seen as the same drink due to their significantly different product methods, ingredients, and geographical requirements. To this day gin and jenever remain two independent spirits, but the latter is still referred to as 'Dutch Gin' due to their entwined history and use of juniper berries.

In the UK 'Old Tom' gin was the preferred version of the drink throughout the 18th century due to its sweeter and softer taste, but the invention of the column still in 1826 made distillation practical, and thus led to the evolution of the 'London Dry' gin that remains popular to this day.

The American Prohibition Era of 1920-33 brought about the production of 'bathtub gin'. This crudely brewed spirit was key in the creation of numerous gin cocktails due to its unpleasant taste- many of the cocktails you'll find in the following pages were created to hide the foul taste of bathtub gin. Bathtub gin isn't actually a real gin classification, merely an attempted emulation of the popular spirit, and so most home-brewed liquor during this period bears this name.

As this brief history shows, the popularity of gin has been unstable over the centuries- few drinks have two of their own laws and a 40-year historical period named after them! Over the 20th century the popularity of gin steadily declined, initially in the 1950's following on from World War II, and then as the decades progressed and drink options grew gin simply failed to keep up with changing market tastes… until now.

Remember the 1751 Gin Act? Well the British government only repealed that in 2008 following a two-year legal battle, so for 257 years it was still illegal to operate a small-scale gin distillery. Following in the footsteps of the craft beer boom of the 2000's craft *gin* distilleries could now operate, and from then on gin was **in**! In 2008 there was one working gin distillery in London- by 2018 there were 24, and the number of British gin brands had more than doubled in the same period. This gin resurrection in the United Kingdom has paved the way for a global rise in gin's popularity. There are now more brands, more flavours, more accessibility, more cocktails, and more fans of gin than ever before!

The modern revival of gin is just another twist in a story spanning 8 centuries- from medicine, to mother's ruin, to our current modern revival, gin has had many bumps in the road. But from here the gin market continues to evolve and offer exceedingly sophisticated and exciting varieties of the traditional juniper infused spirit.

# THE GIN DISTILLERY PROCESS

Gin is made up of 3 components:
An ethanol base spirit
Botanical natural flavourings (juniper being the primary botanical)
And water to dilute the infused spirit to a drinkable ABV level

All gin starts with a neutral base spirit of at least 96% ABV, and by law this spirit must come from agricultural origins. Fermentation of grains (eg. rye or wheat) is the most common way of obtaining the base spirit, however experimentation with grapes or molasses is on the rise as craft breweries continue to push traditional boundaries on their quest for the most daring and unique market offerings. Many breweries will buy this base spirit ready made (pharmaceutical companies are a big producer when it comes to sourcing such highly concentrated alcohol) because it is the distillation (and redistillation) and infusion that is key in the gin making process.

Distillation is an evolving process, for as gin continues to grow in popularity new methods of production are created and refined. There are three main methods of botanical infusion, and these are distilled or one-shot, concentrate, and cold-compound- the quality of gin produced will inevitably vary depending upon the method used. We go into them in detail below, for these processes are essential to turn an alcoholic spirit into the flavourful drink this book is dedicated to.

## DISTILLED // ONE-SHOT

The most laborious and costly method of infusion when producing gin is the classical process known as either 'distilled' or 'one-shot'. This involves taking a base solution of fermented sugar water or a neutral spirit, and infusing it with botanicals. Varieties of the one-shot process are:

### Steeping
'Steeping' was the original method when it came to flavour infusion. This process involves the use of pot stills- an apparatus consisting of a boiler, a condenser, and a connecting vapour path. Ethanol in the boiler is heated, creating a vapour that collects and condenses in the condenser to form a potent alcoholic base. The botanicals are then added to this base and left to steep for a couple of days, therefore infusing the alcohol as it concentrates. The final stage involves the addition of water to dilute the now flavoured base in order to lower ABV levels and create a drinkable spirit.

### Vapour Infusion
Another method is through 'vapour infusion'. This process starts similarly to the steeping one with the use of a pot still to boil and then condense ethanol, but instead of adding the botanicals to the base after they are hung above the boiling liquid. As the ethanol boils it heats the botanicals, and this in turn releases their natural oils. The oils infuse the vapour passes through the botanicals from the boiler to the condenser, therefore creating more delicate and floral notes to the final product.

### Vacuum Distillation
The newest method of infusion is through 'vacuum distillation'. The distillation temperature is lowered for this process in order to prevent excessive breakdown of the botanical essences. The

result is a more layered flavour profile that allows the individual botanicals to be distinguished between more easily.

## Aging

In contrast to the development of new infusion methods, the old method of 'aging' is making a resurgence. Like with other spirits such as whiskey or scotch the gin is left to age in oak barrels. For a richer flavour barrels that had previously stored vermouth or scotch are used, but regardless of the barrel's history the result of this process is a gin featuring a smokier and sharper flavour that permeates throughout other botanical infusions.

## CONCENTRATE

The concentrate method has the exact same premise as a fruit squash: a highly concentrated flavour in a small amount of liquid that can be diluted with ease. Distillers will use one of the one-shot methods to infuse a small amount of base liquid with their botanical mix, but use a disproportionately high quantity of botanicals. The result is a distillate that is highly concentrated with the flavour infusion, and this concentrate will then be diluted with water or neutral spirit.

This process is an economical one; fewer stills are needed for continuous production, and the chance of a 'bad' or irregular batch is drastically reduced. Gin can be produced quickly, and the concentrate enables a more uniform end result.

## COLD-COMPOUND

Cold-compounding is cheap and easy; an agriculturally produced neutral spirit is flavoured with artificial or real botanical essences, and providing the main flavour is that of juniper berries it will pass as gin. This method takes advantage

of the loosest definitions of gin to generate maximum profit and easiest production.

# THE DIFFERENT TYPES OF GIN

We've already mentioned the different definitions and types of gin, but the officially recognised categories of gin are explained in detail below, with each having unique characteristics and individual classification requirements.

## London Dry

The 'typical' gin, most of the brands you'll see on supermarket shelves will fall under the category of a London Dry gin. The taste of juniper is particularly dominant in London Dry gin, and this is because the main classification for a gin of this kind is no additional or artificial flavourings other than those obtained through the botanical infusion stage.

## Plymouth

Although Plymouth gin is a category in its own right there is only one producer of this gin variety- the Black Friars distillery. Drier and more citrussy than London Dry, Plymouth gin contains a unique botanical blend with 7 different components. In production since 1793, the distillery is one of the oldest in the UK. The gin also has strong ties to the British Navy, with a 'navy strength' version of 57% ABV.

## Old Tom

The choice gin of the 18th century, Old Tom gin is sweeter than London Dry, but drier than Genever, whilst maintaining the malt flavour found within the latter. This gin variety had almost died out, but it has experienced a resurgence in line with the 21st century gin revolution- many mixologists find that the sweeter taste works well in cocktails to complement more experimental flavours.

### Genever
Whilst we made it clear in our 'History of Gin' that Genever and gin are two separate drinks, under the definition of gin being a spirit of at least ABV 37.5% with juniper as the predominant flavour, Genever does fall under the gin classification (as the colloquial name 'Dutch Gin' indicates).

Genever is flavoured with juniper and botanicals, but the flavour is weaker than with the other gin categories. Malt wine spirit is used instead of a neutral grain spirit, and so Genever is richer and earthier than its counterparts, and often caramel in colour. In fact, some will describe this gin variation as the bridge between gin and whiskey, and the production process contains steps present in both.

### Sloe
The distinctive floral flavouring and red colouring of sloe gin immediately sets it apart from other gin varieties. Sloe gin is made by typically adding sloes- a small stone fruit similar to plum- to an already made gin and leaving it to infuse. With a lower ABV of 15-30%, this gin variety is on the rise as a milder alternative to its clear counterparts, and numerous US distilleries have taken up production with added twists on the traditional sloe, such as plums and locally produced fruits.

### International Style
These are the new age gins born from the current gin revolution! International style gins keep the traditional neutral spirit base and predominant juniper flavour but introduce other botanicals for a more flavoursome and aromatic final product.

These styles of gin are popular to use in cocktails because of the extra layers of flavour.

**Navy Strength**

Navy strength gin is very similar to London dry when it comes to flavour profiles but packing a much stronger punch! With ABV levels of 57% this gin is best suited to intensely flavoured cocktails due to its ability to maintain a strong juniper presence. Navy gin gets its name from the 18th century tradition of gunpowder being doused in gin and then lit- if the gunpowder burned cleanly then the gin was of a suitable quality and strength!

# THE BEST GIN BRANDS TO TRY IN 2020

In comparison to just a decade ago, the rise in numbers of gin brands is extraordinary. The market is not only booming with fresh new brands, but also new distillation processes, new favours, and a whole new culture of gin appreciation. There's now so many choices out there that settling on only one bottle is a near impossible task! To help you expand and refine your gin appreciation we've put together a list of the 15 best brands to try in 2020. This list takes you all around the globe and offers countless new and exciting flavours; from the award winning to the relatively unknown, give these brands a try and never look back.

### Hendricks
Originates from Ayrshire, Scotland
Alcohol levels 41.4%
Known for its unique flavouring Hendricks classic gin, flavoured with cucumber and rose, has unwavering popularity within the gin community. Fantastical, unusual, and eccentric; the branding of this gin is perfectly in line with the uniquely flavoured and distilled allure of Hendricks.

### Sipsmith
Originates from London, UK
Alcohol levels 41.6%
The Sipsmith distillery led the 2008 legal reforms that now permit small scale gin production in the UK. Their production method was the first to feature copper stills in 200 years, and

the resurrection of this distillery process in combination with the legalising of microbreweries was a huge factor in the gin revolution that continues to develop.

### Monkey 47
Originates from Black Forest, Germany
Alcohol levels 47%
47% alcohol and 47 botanical flavourings give this gin its numerical name. Some of the flavours used within those impressive 47 include honey, almonds, six different types of pepper, pomelo, and lingonberries.

### LoneWolf
Originates from Ellon, Scotland
Alcohol levels 40%
A true ode to gin with its strong juniper taste, LoneWolf is the Brewdog Distillery's line of gin. Original, cloudy lemon, and cactus and lime flavours are available, but all stick pack a juniper punch. The original is distinct with fragrant notes of lavender and citrus and serves as the base for LoneWolf's more experimental gin products.

### Lind and Lime Gin
Originates from Edinburgh, Scotland
Alcohol level 44%
The Port of Leigh Distillery created their first gin with Dr James Lind- the doctor who discovered that the vitamin C citrus fruits are packed with helped cure scurvy- as their inspiration. Though their gin may not quite count as medicine, the balance of lime to juniper is a tribute to Dr Lind, with other botanicals like pink peppercorn subtly rounding off the zesty flavour.

### Dingle Gin
Originates from County Kerry, Ireland
Alcohol levels 42.5%
There were 400 other gin competitors, but it was Dingle Gin's offering that was the winner at the World Gin Awards following a blind taste test. Their use of local botanicals to infuse their gin has resulted in a highly sophisticated drink that a perfect balance between floral and fresh flavours.

### Tanqueray No.10
Originates from London, UK
Alcohol levels 43.7%
One of the classics, you can never go wrong with Tanqueray No.10. Production of this gin started over in 1830, and 170 years later it is the globally top selling gin brand. The iconic green bottle with red wax crest is synonymous with mainstream, high quality gin.

### Williams Chase gin
Originates from Herefordshire, UK
Alcohol levels 48%
The distillation for this gin takes 2 years due the process being undergone over 100 times. The distillery produces a selection of gins, from their classic Chase GB Gin, to a pink Rhubarb and Bramley Apple number, and a Sloe Gin to name but a few of their products.

### No.209 Gin
Originates from San Francisco, USA
Alcohol levels 46%
The 209th registered distillery in the US, it's no mystery where the brand gets its name from. Featuring a complex flavour profile that includes bergamot, cardamom, coriander, and orange, and a process that involves 5 sets of distillation, the passion this

small-scale brewery puts into production is evident in the quality of the gin they produce.

### Gin Mare
Originates from Costa Brava, Spain
Alcohol levels 42.7%
In a small Spanish 13<sup>th</sup> century chapel you can find gin being infused with the essence of the Mediterranean and bottled. In addition to juniper, olives are a key ingredient in the flavouring of this gin. It is one of the few herbal gins on the market, with notes of rosemary, thyme, and basil enhancing the sun-soaked Mediterranean feeling.

### Martin Miller's Gin
Originates form Black Country, UK
Alcohol levels 40%
Counted as one of the top-shelf, premium gins of the day. Their offering to the gin world has received the most awards of any gin in the last decade, and is the highest scoring gin of the Beverage Testing Institute of Chicago, attaining 97 points in both 2003 and 2015.

### Elephant Gin
Originates from Hamburg, Germany
Alcohol levels 45%
This gin is as delicious as it is philanthropic- from their emergence in 2013 15% of all proceeds have been donated to two African elephant charities. Elephant gin has clear African influences, with unusual ingredients like Devil's Claw and African Wormwood featuring in their sophisticated flavour profile.

### Boodles British Gin
Originates from Warrington, UK
Alcohol levels 45.2%

Boodles Gin purposefully leaves out citrus from its distillation process- a choice that sets its flavour apart from many other gins on the market. Instead, Boodles Gin it takes inspiration from a recipe dated in 1845 where herbs and spices including sage, rosemary and nutmeg are used, with the result being a decidedly aromatic taste that smoothly complements the traditional juniper flavour.

### Glendalough Gin

Originates from Glendalough, Ireland
Alcohol levels 41-44%
As a result of using only locally sourced botanicals to flavour their gin, the Glendalough Gin brewery produces 4 gin varieties a year- one each for spring, summer, autumn, and winter. Whilst the base of their gin is constant the botanical infusions vary in line with the seasons, leading to unique flavour profiles that include ingredients such as dandelion leaves and ground ivy.

### Cruxland Gin

Originate from Paarl, South Africa
Alcohol levels 43%
The only African gin to feature on our list, Cruxland gin stays true to its roots by using traditional South African flavours like Rooibos and Honey Bush to infuse their gin. Their secret ingredient (Kalahari Truffle) creates a full-bodied and earthy flavour, and further boosts the drinks luxury status.

# THE MIXOLOGIST ESSENTIALS

For the cocktails featured the equipment is pretty basic- a jigger, stirrer, strainer, and cocktail shaker are the most any of them really need! But any aspiring mixologist needs to understand the tools of the trade, so kit yourself out with the mixology essentials we've listed below.

### A jigger

A jigger is the most important item a mixologist can have. The recipes this book contains use ounces / oz. as a measurement, and a jigger is the tool used to perfect such measurements. Mixology is a precise art- cocktails are not just a mishmash of what someone suspects will taste nice! Having on hand a two-sided ½//1½ oz. jigger will allow you to quickly mix up your cocktail with exact measurements, and as your skills progress more jiggers of varying measurement may be needed.

### A cocktail shaker

When you think of a cocktail you undoubtedly conjure up the image of a bartender shaking up a drink with a bit of pizzazz. You can choose between Boston Shakers, Cobbler Cocktail Shakers, Parisian Shakers, Toby Tins and beyond, but whichever style of cocktail shaker you decide upon this item is priceless to ensure your drinks are mixed, chilled, and delivered in style.

### A strainer

Your chosen shaker may have a strainer built in, but if it doesn't then the purchasing of a good quality strainer will be an imme-

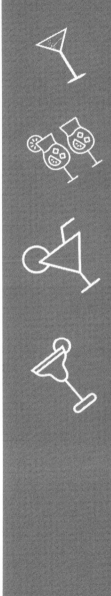

diate priority. The strainer is used to remove any ice, pulp, or other unwanted extras that may add flavour, but are no longer required. Popular strainers include the Hawthorne and Julep styles.

### A bar spoon

Contrary to what you may have assumed a bar spoon is a specialised tool to elevate a cocktail's creation. The spoon measures 1tsp, thus making it handy to add strong flavours with care, and the neck of the spoon is long and twisted. This twisted feature is what really sets a bar spoon apart from any other teaspoon- by twisting when mixing the drink experiences minimal disturbance which allows artistic drink layer or shaken aeration to remain intact.

### A muddler

A less essential (but still very important) tool, the muddler is used to prepare ingredients like herbs- the muddler gently massages the ingredient to release its natural oils and flavour without damaging it in the process

### A juicer

If you're able to use fresh juice in your cocktails then do it- fresh juice will always create a superior drink to one that uses a bottled mixer. You may already have a juicer hanging around, so put it to good use and get the pulp flowing!

### A channel knife

This oddly shaped contraption is designed to remove strips of rind without catching the pith beneath. For decorative peel twists the channel knife is key for both its style and its simplicity.

A strainer, muddler, juicer, bar spoon, and channel knife can be improvised to a degree so don't fret! For the cocktails we've included in this book the two key pieces of equipment are a jigger and a cocktail shaker, so before you start have those on hand to avoid any mixology mishaps!

# COCKTAILS GLASSES

So, you've got the equipment, whipped up a top class cocktail, and then what? Pour it into your everyday drinking glass?! Cocktail glasses aren't just there to look nice- they're designed for practical reasons like aeration and temperature regulation. Every cocktail will have a preferred glass and we've indicated in the cocktail recipes which is best for the particular drink- find out more about each of the glasses you'll encounter below.

## COUPE
More rounded and smaller than a martini glass, a coupe glass will generally hold 6 oz. of liquid. This glass is used for cocktails that aren't served with ice (they will have been sufficiently chilled in the mixing process), hence the long stem. Their open shape also allows easy smelling for when aroma is a crucial part of the beverage experience.

## MARTINI
The iconic V shape of this glass is associated with cocktails and class globally. As the name says, this glass was designed to serve martinis, but its use has grown to a wide range of cocktails. Like the coupe glass the martini was designed to avoid heating drinks that are not served with ice.

## OLD-FASHIONED
Also known as a lowball, rocks, or double-rocks glass, this robust glass has many purposes. Used for straight liquor or muddled cocktails (the thick base is a design feature to allow muddling in the glass itself) the old-fashioned glass tends to hold 6-8 oz., and the double-rocks variation will hold 12-16oz. The

thick base also helps with heat regulation whether a drink is served on the rocks/ with ice, or without.

### HIGHBALL

The highball and Collins glasses are essentially interchangeable- the only difference is that the Collins is a fraction taller. A 12 oz. glass is ideal for cocktails that contain a large amount of mixer, or where lots of ice is used.

### GOBLET

Designed to act as an 'all-purpose' receptacle, the goblet looks like an enlarged wine glass in many ways. Goblets are versatile, allowing for larger quantities of drink or the addition of ice, and with a shorter stem that still allows temperature regulation, but is sturdier for practicalities.

### CHAMPAGNE FLUTE

The champagne flute's high surface area to volume ratio prevents fizzy drinks like prosecco and champagne from going flat too quickly. The small mouth encourages drinkers to slowly sip, and the long body also serves a decorative purpose if other ingredients are added to the straight drink or cocktail.

# FANCY MAKING YOUR OWN GIN?

It's surprisingly easy to create a batch of home distilled gin! The easiest method of doing this is through 'steeping' (placing your botanicals into the heated neutral base spirit and leaving them to infuse). Botanicals are the magic ingredient when it comes to making your own gin, and we've included a recipe below featuring some common botanicals used to infuse gin but be sure to experiment with other flavours and measurements until you've found your perfect mix.

- 750ml vodka

- 2 tbsp juniper berries, frozen

- 4 cardamom pods

- 1 tsp dried rose petals

- 2 strips dried orange peel

- 2 strips dried lemon peel

1. In a large saucepan gently heat your vodka. You want it to be too hot to touch but not boiling.

2. Whilst the vodka heats place your juniper berries, cardamom pods, and dried rose petals into a heavy bottomed glass or bowl and gently muddle.

3. Remove your vodka from the heat and leave to cool for 5-10 minutes before pouring in your muddled mixture, dried orange peel, and dried lemon peel. Stir and leave to cool fully.

4. Once cooled pour everything into a sterilised container. Leave in a cool, dark place for 24 hours.

5. After 24 hours taste the mixture. If it is infused to your liking then strain the liquid into another sterilised container, being sure to remove all botanicals. If not infused enough then shake and leave for another 2-4 hours before repeating the tasting process.

6. If there is any remaining sediment pour the liquid through a muslin or coffee filter.

7. Store your gin in a cool dark place and enjoy on the rocks with tonic water to fully experience your infusion

Other flavourings you could experiment with include:

- Black or pink peppercorns

- Lavender

- Star Anise

- Cucumber

- Cinnamon

- Orris root

- Angelica root

- Coriander

- Nutmeg

- Mint

- Liquorice root

- Almond

- Lemongrass

- Bay leaf

- Dried citrus peel eg. grapefruit, lime, kumquat

# GIN COCKTAILS

*All of the recipes featured include measurements for the mixing of one cocktail, but this can easily be adapted for larger batches, where 1 oz. = 30ml*

# GIN AND TONIC

## *Highball*

*The iconic gin and tonic was developed by the British East India Company in the early years of the 19$^{th}$ century for troops in India- tonic water was already being mixed with quinine to make the anti-malarial medication more bearable, but in adding gin the drink moved from 'bearable' to 'enjoyable'*

Y 2 oz. gin

Y 3-4 oz. tonic water

Y 2 lime wedges

Y 2 ice cubes

1. Place your ice cubes into your glass and pour over your gin.

2. Pour in your tonic water. The general ration is 1:3, but feel free to add more or less in order to suit your strength preference.

3. Squeeze in the juice of one lime wedge and stir to mix.

4. Garnish with your remaining lime wedge.

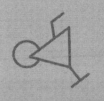

# GIMLET

## *Martini*

*The mixing of lime with gin started off for medical reasons—the vitamin C found in citrus fruits helped sailors avoid developing scurvy on long sea voyages, and lime and gin turned out to be a match made in Heaven!*

- 4 oz. gin
- ½ oz. fresh lime juice + ½ oz. simple syrup
- OR
- 1 oz. lime cordial (traditionally Rose's)
- 2 ice cubes
- Lime ribbon to garnish

1. Before starting be sure to chill your glass in the fridge for 5 minutes.

2. Place your gin, lime cordial, and ice cubes into a cocktail shaker.

3. Shake everything for 10 seconds and then strain into your chilled glass.

4. Garnish with a lime ribbon.

# GIN FIZZ

## *Highball*

The 'fizz' cocktail family is simply a mixed cocktail consisting of a spirit, citrus fruit juice, and carbonated water. The gin fizz is the most well known member of this cocktail group, but other offerings using whiskey and rum are similarly delightful

- Y 2 oz. gin
- Y ¾ oz. lemon juice
- Y ¾ oz. simple syrup
- Y Optional 1 egg white
- Y 2 oz. soda water
- Y 4 ice cubes
- Y Lemon twist to garnish

1. Place your gin, lemon juice, simple syrup, 2 ice cubes, and optional egg white into a cocktail shaker.

2. Shake vigorously for 20-30 seconds, taking longer if using an egg white to ensure all the ingredients are thoroughly combined.

3. Strain the mixture into your glass, being sure to place your remaining 2 ice cubes in the receptacle prior to adding your shaken mixture.

4. Top up the glass with soda water, and garnish with a lemon twist.

# NEGRONI

## *Old-Fashioned*

*The marmite of the cocktail world, some love the bitter aperitif that is a negroni, and some can't stomach it. In 2013 a global week of charity – 'Negroni Week'- was started to pay homage to this classic drink and raise money whilst doing so*

- 🍸 1 oz. dry gin

- 🍸 1 oz. sweet vermouth

- 🍸 1 oz. Campari

- 🍸 2 ice cubes

- 🍸 Orange peel to garnish

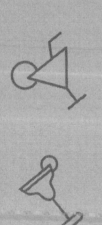

1. Before starting be sure to chill your glass in the fridge for 5 minutes.

2. Place all your ingredients (except the orange peel garnish) into your now chilled old-fashioned glass.

3. Stir everything together and then serve, garnishing with the orange peel.

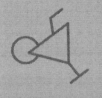

# MARTINI

## *Martini*

*The martini is surrounded by conflicting ideas- shaken or stirred? Vodka or gin? Dry vermouth or sweet vermouth? The original martini is a stirred cocktail containing gin and equal parts dry to sweet vermouth, and it is the product of this combination that is revered globally*

- Y 2 ½ oz. dry gin

- Y ½ oz. dry vermouth

- Y Cracked ice

- Y Stuffed green olive and 2 lemon twists for garnish

1. Before starting be sure to chill your glass in the fridge for 5 minutes.

2. Place your gin, dry vermouth, and ice into a large glass or a cocktail shaker and stir with a bar spoon for 10-15 seconds, then strain into your chilled martini glass.

3. Squeeze your lemon twist over the drink to express the peel's oil, then wipe the peel around the rim of the glass.

4. Garnish with the remaining peel and a stuffed green olive.

# PINK GIN

## *Coupe*

Designed to be mixed using Plymouth gin, the pink gin cocktail gained popularity in the 19th century, and was initially a medicinal naval drink. Angostura bitters were used to treat seasickness, so by mixing them with gin an enjoyable remedy was available

Ɏ 2 oz. gin

Ɏ 3-4 drops angostura bitters

Ɏ 3 ice cubes

Ɏ 2 Lemon twists to garnish

1. Place your gin, angostura bitters, and ice cubes into a large glass or a cocktail shaker.

2. Stir for 10-20 seconds to ensure everything is combined and chilled- the drink should mix to a pink hue and the glass or cocktail shaker will have cooled during this process.

3. Strain into your glass and squeeze over one lemon peel to express the natural oils, then use the other peel as a garnish.

# SINGAPORE SLING

## *Highball*

A bartender in the Raffles Hotel's Long Bar created the Singapore Sling in 1915. It was deemed unsightly for a woman to drink alcohol in public at that time, and so the drink was created to appear as a fruit juice in order to hide the alcoholic kick female patrons were now able to enjoy

- 1 ½ oz. gin
- 1 oz. Benedictine
- 1 oz. lime juice
- ½ oz. cherry liqueur
- ¼ oz. simple syrup
- 8 ice cubes
- 2 oz. club soda
- Maraschino cherry and a lime or lemon slice to garnish

1. Place your gin, Benedictine, lime juice, cherry liqueur, simple syrup, and 4 ice cubes into a cocktail shaker.

2. Shake well for 10-20 seconds to ensure everything is combined.

3. Strain into a highball glass containing your remaining 4 ice cubes, before topping up with your club soda.

4. Garnish with a maraschino cherry and slice of lime or lemon.

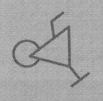

# TOM COLLINS

## *Highball*

The Tom Collins and fizz cocktail family are first referenced in a 1882 mixology book, although it is likely they predate the publication. The original Tom Collins specifies using Old Tom gin, and a variation called a John Collins calls for the use of Dutch Gin (genever)

- ⟁ 2 oz. dry gin

- ⟁ 1 oz. lemon juice

- ⟁ ½ oz. simple syrup

- ⟁ 2 oz. club soda

- ⟁ Maraschino cherry and lemon twist to garnish

1. Before starting be sure to chill your glass in the fridge for 5 minutes.

2. Remove the glass from the fridge and pour in your gin, lemon juice, and simple syrup, then stir to combine.

3. Top up with club soda before serving garnished with a maraschino cherry and lemon twist.

# THE LAST WORD

## *Coupe*

The first recipe for this cocktail was published in 1951, but it is made clear that The Last Word was a popular prohibition-era cocktail that was first mixed in the 1920's at a Detroit athletics club- the drink is 100% carbohydrate and so would certainly provide an energy boost post-training!

- ¾ oz. gin
- ¾ oz. green chartreuse
- ¾ oz. maraschino liqueur
- ¾ oz. lime juice
- 3 ice cubes

1. Before starting be sure to chill your glass in the fridge for 5 minutes.

2. Place all the ingredients into a cocktail shaker.

3. Shake for 15-20 seconds, then double strain the liquid into your chilled coupe glass and serve.

# VESPER

## *Martini*

*Modelled on the martinin, the vesper adds ectra dimension with the addition of vodka an aromatised wine instead of vermouth. Named after Vesper, a lover of James Bond, the drink is specified in Casino Royale as an alternative to the controversial 'shaken not stirred' martini*

Y 1 ½ oz. gin

Y 1 oz. vodka

Y ½ oz. lillet blanc

Y 4 ice cubes

Y 2 lemon twists

1. Pour your gin, vodka, and lillet blanc into a large glass or a cocktail shaker containing your ice cubes.

2. Stir with a bar spoon for 30 seconds so everything is fully combined and chilled, then strain into your glass.

3. Squeeze one of your lemon twists over your drink to express the oil, then wipe around the rim of the glass.

4. Garnish with the remaining lemon twist to serve.

# AVIATION

## Coupe

*A beautifully lilac hued cocktail, the Aviation was developed by a German bartender and published in pre-prohibition America in 1916. The simplicity of the ingredients tend to lull the mixer into a false sense of safety- the delicate flavour balance can easily be disturbed and the drinker may think they are sipping on grandmother's perfume by mistake*

- 2 oz. gin
- ½ oz. maraschino liqueur
- ½ oz. crème de violette
- ¾ oz. lemon juice
- 3 ice cubes
- Brandied cherry to garnish

1. Place all your ingredients into a cocktail shaker.

2. Shake for 30 seconds in order to thoroughly combine and chill all ingredients.

3. Strain into a coupe glass and then garnish with a brandied cherry to serve.

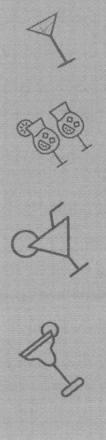

# FRENCH 75

## *Champagne flute*

*Similar to the Tom Collins, the French 75 uses champagne as a mixer instead of carbonated water or juices. The drink gained popularity in the mid-20th century when references to the cocktail in famous films like Casablanca and A Man Betrayed emphasised its luxury status*

- Ⓨ 2 oz. dry gin

- Ⓨ ¾ oz. lemon juice

- Ⓨ ¾ oz. simple syrup

- Ⓨ 2 oz. Champagne

- Ⓨ 4 ice cubes

- Ⓨ Lemon twist to garnish

1. Place your gin, lemon juice, simple syrup, and ice cubes into a cocktail shaker.

2. Shake vigorously for 30 seconds.

3. Strain your drink into your glass before topping up the flute with champagne.

4. Serve with your lemon twist as garnish.

The following cocktails are not classified as classical gin cocktails, but mixes like the Ginger Rogers are gaining popularity and recognition in the new age gin revolution. We haven't specified the use of specially flavoured gins, but some of these cocktails work well with particularly citrussy or aromatic offerings- get experimental to familiarise yourself with complementary flavours and different gin variations.

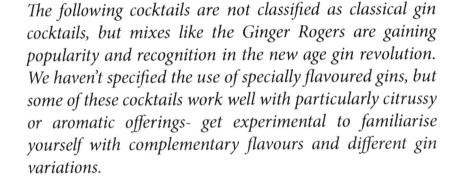

# THE GINGER ROGERS

## *Highball*

- ½ oz. ginger syrup
- 2 oz. grapefruit juice
- 1 oz. lemon juice
- 1 ½ oz. gin
- 2 oz. soda water
- 4 ice cubes
- Rosemary to garnish

1. Place all your ingredients minus the soda water into a cocktail shaker.

2. Shake vigorously for 20 30 seconds.

3. Strain into your glass and then top up with soda water.

4. Garnish with rosemary to serve.

# FIG AND VANILLA BEAN COCKTAIL

## *Old-fashioned*

- 🍸 1 ½ oz. gin
- 🍸 ½ oz. fig and vanilla bean syrup (recipe below)
- 🍸 2 dashes orange bitters
- 🍸 3 oz. tonic water
- 🍸 4 ice cubes
- 🍸 Fresh fig to garnish

1. Place your gin, flavoured syrup, orange bitters, and 3 ice cubes into a large glass or cocktail shaker.

2. Stir with a bar spoon to ensure ingredients are thoroughly mixed.

3. Place your remaining ice cube into your glass and strain your mixed drink over it.

4. Top up with tonic water, then garnish with a fresh fig to serve

# SYRUP

## *(yields 6 oz.)*

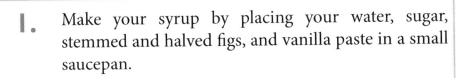

Y ½ c water

Y ½ c sugar

Y 6 fresh figs

Y 1 tsp vanilla paste

**1.** Make your syrup by placing your water, sugar, stemmed and halved figs, and vanilla paste in a small saucepan.

**2.** Turn the heat to high until the mixture reaches a rolling boil, then reduce heat and leave to simmer, stirring frequently.

**3.** The syrup will be ready once the figs are softened and easily breaking- remove from the heat at this point.

**4.** Leave to cool before sieving into an airtight container.

**5.** This syrup will keep in the fridge for up to a week.

# THE WITCHING HOUR

*Coupe*

- 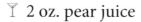 2 oz. pear juice

- 1 oz. dry gin

- ½ oz. chartreuse liqueur

- 4 tsp lemon juice

- ¼ tsp activated charcoal powder

- 4 ice cubes

- 1 dried sage leaf to garnish

1. Before starting be sure to chill your glass in the fridge for 5 minutes.

2. Place all ingredients minus the sage leaf into a cocktail shaker.

3. Shake vigorously for 30 seconds to thoroughly combine and chill all ingredients, then pour into your chilled glass.

4. Use a lighter or match to set the sage leaf alight and then drop the burning leaf into your drink. Serve immediately whilst the leaf is still smoking.

# MIDNIGHT SPARKLER

*Coupe*

- 1 oz. crème de violette
- ½ oz. orange juice
- ½ oz. lemon juice
- ½ oz. gin
- 3 ice cubes
- 3 oz. Champagne
- Lemon twist, lemon slice, and sanding sugar to garnish

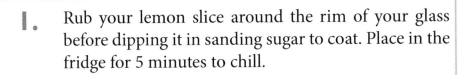

1. Rub your lemon slice around the rim of your glass before dipping it in sanding sugar to coat. Place in the fridge for 5 minutes to chill.

2. Place your ice cubes, crème de violette, orange juice, lemon juice, and gin into a cocktail shaker.

3. Shake vigorously for 30 seconds, then strain into your chilled and frosted coupe glass.

4. Top up with Champagne and garnish with your lemon twist to serve.

# LELAND PALMER

*Highball*

- Y 1 tbsp honey
- Y 1 tbsp hot water
- Y 3 oz. cooled jasmine tea
- Y 1 oz. gin
- Y 1 oz. limoncello
- Y 1 oz. lemon juice
- Y ¾ oz. grapefruit juice
- Y 1 ½ oz club soda
- Y 2 ice cubes
- Y Lemon slice to garnish

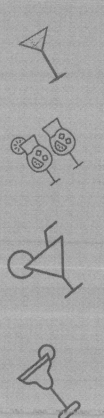

1. Create a quick simple syrup by mixing together your honey and hot water, and then leave it to cool.

2. Once it has cooled combine your honey mix with the remaining ingredients by placing all into your glass and stirring together.

3. Top up with club soda then garnish with a lemon slice to serve.

# RASPBERRY-ROSE GIN RICKEY

## *Old-fashioned*

- Handful of fresh raspberries

- 2 oz. gin

- 1 tsp sugar

- 1 oz. lime juice

- 1 drop rosewater

- 1 oz. tonic water

- 3 tbsp crushed ice

- Lime twist to garnish

1. Use a fork to crush your raspberries in a bowl.

2. Add your sugar, lime juice, and rosewater to the crushed berries and then stir everything to combine.

3. Transfer the raspberry mix to your glass before adding your crushed ice, gin, and tonic water.

4. Stir everything to ensure all ingredients are combined and chilled.

5. Serve with a lime twist as garnish.

# AUTUMN GIN SOUR

*Coupe*

- Y 1 ½ oz. gin
- Y ¾ oz. lemon juice
- Y ½ oz. grand marnier
- Y 1 tsp orange marmalade
- Y ½ an egg white
- Y 4 ice cubes

1. Before starting be sure to place your glass in the fridge to cool for 5 minutes.

2. If desired set aside one ice cube for an extra chilled serving and then place all your remaining ingredients into a cocktail shaker.

3. Shake vigorously for 1 minute to create a chilled, combined, and frothy mixture.

4. Strain your drink into your chilled glass and if desired use the remaining ice cube to keep your drink extra cool.

# SAINT-FLORENT

*Goblet*

- ▼ 1 tbsp honey
- ▼ 1 tbsp hot water
- ▼ 1 ½ oz. gin
- ▼ ¾ oz. lime juice
- ▼ ½ oz. Aperol
- ▼ 2 dashes of Angostura bitters
- ▼ 2 ice cubes
- ▼ 2 oz. Champagne
- ▼ Lime twist to garnish

1. Start by dissolving your honey in the hot water and setting aside to cool for a few minutes in order to create a quick simple syrup.

2. Place this honey syrup in a cocktail shaker and pour over your gin, lime juice, Aperol, Angostura bitters, and ice cubes.

3. Shake vigorously for 30 seconds before straining into your glass.

4. Top up with Champagne and garnish with your lime twist to serve.

# THE GIBSON

## *Martini*

- 🍸 2 oz. gin
- 🍸 ½ oz. blanc vermouth
- 🍸 ½ oz. dry vermouth
- 🍸 ¼ oz. juice from a pickled onion jar
- 🍸 2 cups of crushed ice
- 🍸 Pickled onion to serve

**1.** Pour your crushed ice into a shaker- you want the shaker to be full, so more ice may be needed.

**2.** Pour in your gin, both vermouths, and pickling liquid.

**3.** Stir for 1- 1½ minutes before straining into your glass – the lengthy stirring is needed for dilution.

**4.** Serve with a pickled onion as garnish.

# MONKEY GLAND

*Coupe*

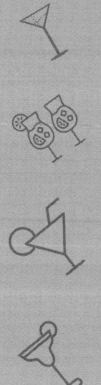

- Ⓨ 2 oz. gin
- Ⓨ 1 oz. orange juice
- Ⓨ ¼ oz. grenadine
- Ⓨ 4 ice cubes
- Ⓨ Dash of absinthe
- Ⓨ Orange slice to garnish

1. Before starting be sure to place your glass in the fridge to chill for 5 minutes.

2. Once chilled, pour your absinthe into the glass. Swirl the liquid around to coat the whole glass, then pour out the excess- the absinthe will have left residue in the glass and it is this residue that is needed for flavouring.

3. Pour your gin, orange juice, grenadine, and ice cubes into a cocktail shaker, and shake for 20 seconds to thoroughly combine.

4. Strain the liquid into your absinthe flavoured glass before garnishing with a slice of orange and serving.

# FLORADORA

*Highball*

- 1 ½ oz. gin
- ½ oz. lime juice
- ½ oz. crème de framboise liqueur
- 4 oz. ginger ale
- 4 ice cubes
- Lime wedge and raspberry to serve

1. Place your ice cubes into the glass and pour over your gin, lime juice, and crème de framboise liqueur.

2. Stir to mix everything together before topping up the glass with your ginger ale.

3. Cut a slit in your lime wedge and rub it around the rim of the glass before setting it as a garnish. Cut up your raspberry and sprinkle it over the drink as a final touch.

It doesn't get more iconic than a gin and tonic. A basic gin and tonic is the first recipe you'll find in this book, and we wanted to finish how we started! Below you'll find some twists on the classic gin and tonic- a perfect encapsulation of how gin has been redefined in recent years by dedicated gin connoisseurs taking a simple gin cocktail drink and elevating it to extraordinary new heights.

*All of the recipes that follow use a highball glass*

# BLUEBERRY AND MINT GIN AND TONIC

- 2 oz. gin
- 3 oz. tonic water
- 1 tbsp fresh lime juice
- 2 mint leaves, chopped
- Handful of fresh or frozen blueberries
- 3 ice cubes
- Mint leaf and lime twist to garnish

**1.** Gently muddle your blueberries in your glass, and once adequately crush stir in your lime juice

**2.** Pour in your ice, gin, tonic water, and mint, then stir to combine and cool

**3.** Serve garnished with a lime twist and additional mint leaf

# ELDERFLOWER AND LEMON GIN AND TONIC

Y 2 oz. gin

Y 3 oz. tonic water

Y 2 tbsp fresh lemon juice

Y ½ oz. elderflower liqueur

Y 3 ice cubes

Y Lemon twist to garnish

1. Place your ice cubes into your glass and pour over your gin, tonic water, lemon juice, and elderflower liqueur

2. Stir thoroughly to combine and cool, then serve garnish with a lime twist

# STRAWBERRY AND BLACK PEPPER GIN AND TONIC

Y 2 oz. gin

Y 3 oz. tonic water

Y 3 fresh strawberries

Y Fresh black pepper

Y 3 ice cubes

**1.** After cutting your strawberries into small piece place them into your glass and gently muddle them

**2.** Use a pepper mill to give 2-3 twists of your black pepper, and muddle again to combine

**3.** Pour in your ice cubes, gin, and tonic water, then stir thoroughly to combine, and serve

# SLOE GIN AND TONIC

- 3 oz. sloe gin
- 3 oz. tonic water
- 1 tbsp fresh lemon juice
- 4 ice cubes
- Lemon twist to garnish

1. Place your gin, tonic water, lemon juice, and 2 ice cubes into a large glass or cocktail shaker, then stir to combine

2. Place your remaining two ice cubes into your glass before straining over your mixed drink

3. Garnish with a lemon twist and serve

# BLOOD ORANGE GIN AND TONIC

- 1 ½ oz. gin
- 2 oz. fresh blood orange juice
- 2-4 dashes orange bitters
- 4 oz. tonic water
- 3 ice cubes
- Blood orange slice to garnish

**1.** Before starting be sure to place your glass in the fridge to chill for 5 minutes

**2.** Place your ice cubes, gin, juice, and orange bitters in your now chilled glass and stir to combine

**3.** Pour over your tonic water and stir gently- you can either fully combine the liquids or only partially

**4.** Garnish with your slice of blood orange and serve

# JAMMY GIN AND TONIC

- Y 1 ½ oz. gin

- Y (preferably Hendricks for the cucumber and rose flavour)

- Y 1 ½ oz. tonic water

- Y 3 tbsp freshly squeezed lemon juice

- Y 1 heaped tbsp jam

- Y (preferably blueberry, but other berry jams will work)

- Y 1 cup crushed ice

- Y 2 ice cubes

- Y Fresh berry garnish

1. Place your crushed ice, gin, tonic water, lemon juice, and jam into a cocktail shaker

2. Shake vigorously for 20-30 seconds to thoroughly combine and chill the ingredients

3. Place your ice cubes into your glass before straining over the shaken cocktail

4. Serve garnished with a fresh berry (preferably in correspondence to your jam!)

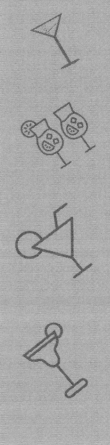

# CHILLI AND LIME GIN AND TONIC

- ⟁ 2 oz. gin

- ⟁ 3 oz. tonic water

- ⟁ 1 red chilli

- ⟁ 2 tbsp fresh lime juice

- ⟁ 2 ice cubes

- ⟁ Lime wedge and salt to garnish

1. Start by running your lime wedge around the rim of your glass. Dip the cup into salt and coat the rim, then set aside

2. Slice and deseed your chilli before placing it in a large glass or cocktail shaker. Gently muddle to release the flavour

3. Pour over the gin, tonic water, and lime juice, then stir with a bar spoon to thoroughly combine

4. Place your ice cubes into the salted glass before straining over your mixed cocktail. Stir gently before serving

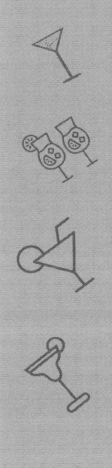

# GRAPEFRUIT AND TARRAGON GIN AND TONIC

- 2 oz. gin
- 4 oz. tonic water
- 2 oz. fresh grapefruit juice
- 1 tbsp honey
- 2 sprigs of tarragon
- 4 ice cubes
- Tarragon sprig and grapefruit slice to garnish

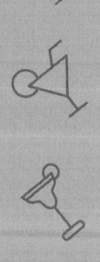

1. Remove the tarragon leaves from your 2 springs and place into a large glass or cocktail shaker. Gently muddle to release the aromatic flavours, then stir in your tablespoon of honey

2. Add in 2 of your ice cubes, gin, tonic water, and grapefruit juice and stir for 30 seconds-1 minute in order to thoroughly combine and infuse

3. Place your remaining 2 ice cubes into your glass before straining over your mixed cocktail

4. Garnish with a tarragon sprig ad grapefruit slice to serve

# GINGER AND STAR ANISE GIN AND TONIC

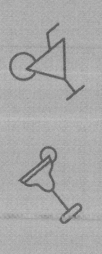

- ⅂ 2 oz. gin
- ⅂ 4 oz. tonic water
- ⅂ 1 orange
- ⅂ 1 star anise
- ⅂ 4 ice cubes
- ⅂ Fresh ginger

1. Start off by taking a potato peeler and peeling thick strips of zest from your orange. Once you have done this to the whole orange cut the flesh into quarters and place these in a cocktail shaker

2. Cut a piece of ginger about 2cm long and cut off the outside. Quarter the ginger and place the quarters into your cocktail shaker

3. Add in your star anise and gin to the cocktail shaker, then put in 2 of your ice cubes and skae vigorously for 20-30 seconds

4. Put your other 2 ice cubes into your glass and strain over the spiced gin. Top up with your tonic water and garnish with the orange peel strips to serve

# COFFEE GIN AND TONIC

- ¥ 1 oz. gin

- ¥ 2 oz. tonic water

- ¥ ½ oz. coffee liqueur

- ¥ 3 ice cubes

- ¥ Lemon zest and a fresh cherry to garnish

1. Place your ice cubes, gin, and coffee liqueur in your glass and stir to combine

2. Top up with your tonic water, stirring once again, before garnishing with lemon zest and a fresh cherry to serve

# IS YOUR GINTEREST PIQUED...?

So, you now know how to define gin, the extensive history of gin, how gin is made, the different gin types, the best brands to try, AND some kick-ass cocktail recipes... do you need anything more? Just in case your gin education hasn't hit the spot yet you can find some interesting, fun, and surprisingly strange facts about gin below- spill some of these over a negroni or vesper and blow the minds of any budding gin enthusiast within ear-shot!

*Did you know...*

At the peak of the Gin Craze in 1721 over 3.5 million gallons of gin were drunk in England

*Did you know...*

When distilling sloe gin the berries' thick skin must be broken in order for the flavour to infuse. Traditionalists argue that the skin must be pricked with a silver needle, but the more practical method is to freeze the berries prior to use which allows the skins to break more easily

*Did you know...*

Despite the name, London Dry gin varieties don't have to be produced in London. In contrast though, a Plymouth gin can only be produced in the Plymouth Black Friars Distillery

*Did you know...*

During the Gin Craze it is estimated that every 1 in 4 London buildings had their own still to produce gin

*Did you know...*

Sir Francis Chichester was the first person to singlehandedly circumnavigate the world in a sailboat. He credited his success to drinking a pink gin cocktail daily

*Did you know...*

The practice of gin distilleries buying a neutral base spirit rather than distilling their own is a legacy from the 1736 Gin Act. This act placed an annual fee equating to £20,000 in todays economy on the production of base spirit, and thc same fee again on the produce of gin

*Did you know...*

Juniper oil acts as a natural flea repellent

*Did you know...*

With its characteristically strong smell, juniper was used during the plague years to ward off the illness. At this time widespread belief was that the plague was transmitted through bad smells

*Did you know...*

Juniper berries are not actually a berry, but in fact a variation on a pinecone

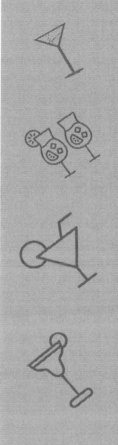

*Did you know...*

The Philippines currently holds the title of highest gin consumption per capita with 43% of global gin market being dominated by Philippine drinkers. These hardcore gin fans even have a term dedicated solely to a gin drinking session- 'Ginuman'

*Did you know...*

When tasting gin it is best to have the liquid at room temperature and diluted with water at a 1:1 ratio in order to properly distinguish the botanical flavourings and distillation quality

*Did you know...*

Gin cocktails with naval origins feature limes rather than lemons because the investors with seats in the British parliament had connections to the Caribbean plantations growing limes

*Did you know...*

There are almost no commercial juniper plantations- nearly all juniper berries used in gin production are picked from the wild

*Did you know...*

A cocktail of gin and tomato juice predates the vodka based Bloody Mary cocktail as a cure for hangovers

*Did you know...*

During the Gin Craze in 1726 there were over 1,500 gin stills in London that were in use, and over 6,000 places to purchase gin (legal and illegal)

*Did you know...*

The Hot Gin Twist was so popular in the winter of 1823 that one passionate drinker wrote a 149 line poem singing praises to the cocktail

*Did you know...*

The martini glass predates the martini cocktail! The glass only gained the name in the 1990's under a martini boom, and before that had simply been titled a cocktail glass

*Did you know...*

Gin is the national spirit of England

*Did you know...*

The term 'Dutch Courage' comes from Dutch soldiers being given gin/ genever before going into battle during the Dutch Independence Wars

*Did you know...*

During the Gin Craze the nickname 'mother's ruin' was given to gin. This was for various reasons, but mainly due to gin often being served in brothels to 'set the mood' for patrons and induce miscarriages for prostitutes

*Did you know...*

The unregulated bathtub gin brewed during the American prohibition era had some lethal side-effects - methanol was sometimes used and drinkers could fall ill and die or face consequences such as blindness

*Did you know...*

Gin is not intended to be drank straight- the complex flavours can only be properly experienced when diluted, hence the classic gin and tonic water pairing

*Did you know...*

Gin based cocktails are the largest spirit based cocktails grouping

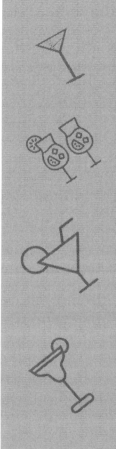

*Did you know...*

There is an annual day dedicated to the celebration of all things gin! Started in 2009, the second Saturday of June marks Global Gin Day for the world over

*Did you know...*

Only in 1970 did British Naval officers stop receiving a daily ration of gin

*Did you know...*

Gin is one of the lower calorie alcoholic drinks available, containing just 54 calories per 25ml

*Did you know...*

Although juniper is a seed it is closely related to the blueberry. Drinking gin can help reduce bloating, help digestion, and fight infection due to the powerful antioxidants contained within juniper berries

*Did you know...*

Up until 2017 it looked like juniper may die out. A fungus was infecting juniper berries and trees so experts stepped in and collected millions of seeds to 'bank', thus ensuring the survival of the plant species

*Did you know...*

Under American prohibition a young man named Theodore Suess Geisel was fired from his job as university newspaper editor after being found smuggling gin into his accommodation. In order to continue his writing he submitted articles under the name 'Suess', and it was from there that Dr Suess began his career as a children's author

*Did you know...*

Jenenver, genever, genièvre, and gin are all derived from the Latin word juniperus

*Did you know...*

Turpentine used to be used to flavour cheap gin in an attempt to mimic the piney notes characteristic of juniper

Printed in Great Britain
by Amazon